I0409614

Survival Family Basics

The Beginner Prepper's Guide for When Disaster Strikes

Macenzie Guiver

© 2013 Healthy Wealthy nWise Press

All Rights Reserved. No part of this publication may be reproduced in any form or by any means, including scanning, photocopying, or otherwise without prior written permission of the copyright holder.

Disclaimer and Terms of Use: The Author and Publisher has strived to be as accurate and complete as possible in the creation of this book, notwithstanding the fact that she does not warrant or represent at any time that the contents within are accurate due to the rapidly changing nature of the Internet. While all attempts have been made to verify information provided in this publication, the Author and Publisher assumes no responsibility for errors, omissions, or contrary interpretation of the subject matter herein. Any perceived slights of specific persons, peoples, or organizations are unintentional. In practical advice books, like anything else in life, there are no guarantees of income made. This book is not intended for use as a source of legal, business, accounting or financial advice. All readers are advised to seek services of competent professionals in legal, business, accounting, and finance field.

Printed in the United States of America

Just to say Thank You for Purchasing this Book I want to give you a gift <u>100% absolutely FREE</u>

A Copy of My Upcoming Special Report *"The Prepper's Supplies Guide for When Disaster Strikes"*

Go to <u>www.SurvivalFamilyBasics.com</u> to Sign Up to Receive Your FREE Gift

Table of Contents

Introduction

I want to thank you and congratulate you for downloading the book, *"Survival Family Basics-Beginner's Prepper's Guide for when Disaster Strikes'*.

The book takes you into the austere regions of your nightmares and provides you with answers to all the questions people are afraid to ask while offering hope, reassurance and encouragement. It is hard to even imagine a time when you have to make some split second decisions in life-decisions that many of us are afraid to make, but the truth is that at some point in life, many of us may be confronted with such situations that force us to make such decisions.

From Rocky Mountain wildfires, to Atlantic hurricanes to California earthquakes, you cannot escape the inevitable day when a disaster or catastrophe strikes your home town. While you cannot escape the inevitable, no matter how hard you may try, you can always take preventive measures to reduce anxiety, fear and losses that accompany disasters.

In addition to providing proven tips and strategies on how to smartly and quickly respond to disasters like earthquakes, fires, hurricanes and floods-how to stay protected from extreme weather and stay calm and composed during these situations, the book contains step by step advice on how to prepare for, respond to and recover from disasters.

From preparing your evacuation plan to the importance of preparing for a disaster, the book includes all the information that you need to know to live safely through the worst. It is aimed at helping you and your family plan for a variety of emergency situations, persevere during these times and recover when it's over.

Why Prepare-The Importance of Preparing for a Disaster

"Being prepared is the best defense against danger"

Disasters often strike without warning and can leave massive destruction and ruin in their wake. You could be forced to go for days without basic necessities or evacuate your home.

Survivors, nevertheless; can get through even the toughest circumstances using the right information and tools. Knowing which type of disasters could affect your area will help you plan more thoroughly for dealing with such situations.

Whilst the advancement in the field of science and technology may lead us to a reasonable understanding of some phenomenon, it does not unfortunately translate into an accurate prediction capability.

Knowing the steps you need to take during an emergency situation can greatly reduce the risk, danger and distress you may face in case you are confronted with such a situation. Knowing that you are prepared to face the worst will definitely help you sleep a little easier at night.

Prepare to face the worst-Disasters are Unpredictable

In the year 1993, the eastern coast of the United States was hit by the 'Storm of the Century' killing hundreds and causing billions of dollars in damage. Spawning tornadoes in Florida and dumping record levels of snowfall across the

Mid-Atlantic States and Appalachian Mountains, the storm resulted in extremely low temperatures throughout the region and produced hurricane-force winds. The snow caused blizzard conditions in the Eastern region of United States bringing life to a sudden halt in many areas.

Figure 1: Storm of the Century-(1993)

In the year, 2005, the Gulf coast of the United States was pounded with devastating force by one of the deadliest hurricanes in the history of the United States-Hurricane Katrina. Packed with sustained winds of 145 mph at landfall, the category-3 storm left more than a million people in three states with submerged highways and power outage. Though the storm itself caused a great deal of destruction, the aftermath was catastrophic.

Figure 2: Hurricane Katrina

Benefits of Prepping For an Emergency Situation:

Disasters disrupt hundreds of thousands of lives each year and leave a trail of devastation in their wake.

Whilst you cannot predict when a disaster will strike, the better you plan when you begin prepping, the better prepared you will be for dealing with such situations. By practicing prevention, the risk of a disaster can be mitigated. Understanding the types of disasters that are likely to affect your area can prove to be of significant help when you are faced with such a situation.

Despite the fact that your local government and disaster relief organizations will try to help you in the event of an emergency situation they may not be able to reach you immediately. By preparing yourself in advance for an emergency situation, you can enjoy the following benefits;

1. Taking preventive measures to deal with an emergency situation can reduce anxiety, fear and losses that accompany disasters.
2. Preparing in advance for an emergency situation can also reduce the impact of disasters and alleviate the risk.
3. Additionally, preparing well in advance for an emergency situation is important to surviving and recovering from a disaster.
4. It is important that you have the right knowledge to respond to disasters that could hit your area, - power outages, storms, tornadoes, hurricanes, extreme weather conditions, terrorism or flooding. It is important that you prepare yourself for at least three days in case the emergency help is delayed.
5. In addition, taking a CPR/AED course or a first aid course is essential to preparing yourself well for an emergency situation.

Getting Informed-Know What You are Preparing For

When the earth shakes, a tornado strikes, a plane crashes or a storm hits, the survivors are viewed as the lucky ones. Had they been in the hotel across the street or in the unlucky airplane, they would have been perished. We are awestruck at the whimsy of the catastrophe. However, survival is not merely a product of fate.

It goes without saying that no one can predict what fate has in store for them, but when unexpected events occur-from a fire outbreak to flooding, to a terrorist attack, it does pay to prepare. People when caught in chaos are barely able to decide anything. They are confused, scared and anxious for clear direction.

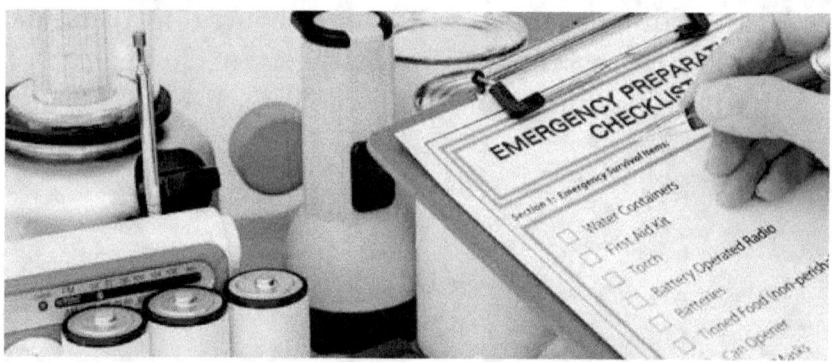

If a disaster strikes today, would you know what to do? You could be forced to evacuate your neighborhood or a certain situation may confine you to your home. What would you do if you are confined to your home without basic services such as electricity, water and gas? Would you be able to survive if these services were cut off? Whilst local relief workers and emergency teams respond quickly in these situations, everyone cannot be helped right away.

You could be anywhere when a disaster hits your area- in your car, at work or may be at your home. How are you going to know if your family is safe? These are important questions that need some serious answers.

Be Informed

Learning about the hazards that may hit your area, may help you cope with the situation in a much better manner. This information can be obtained from the office of local emergency management or the local American Red Cross Chapter.

- You need to ask what types of disasters are most likely to hit your area. Additionally, request information on how to plan for each of these. (Use the worksheet given later in the book to record your findings and suggestions for reducing the risk to your family).
- If you have a medical condition that requires you to use certain medical equipment (that requires electricity to function), you need to get information about what to do when there is a power outage.
- Additionally, if you undergo routine treatment at a hospital or clinic, or if you receive regular health care services such as physical therapy services, talk to your medical service provider about their emergency plans.
- It is also important for you to be informed about the disaster plans at your workplace or your child's school.
- If you own a pet, you also need to be informed about animal care after a disaster.

Whilst different situations call for different strategies and plans, such as assembling an emergency supply kit and making an emergency plan are the same or universal-irrespective of the type of emergency. Nevertheless, it is important to be informed about what types of emergencies are likely to affect your area. Creating a plan that fits your needs before, during and after a disaster will help you be more self-sufficient in an emergency situation and stay focused and composed.

Specific Disasters Crisis-Preparation and Strategies

Natural Disasters

Fire

More than 4,000 Americans die each year, and thousands of them are injured in fire outbreaks- fire outbreaks which could have been prevented. Property losses due to these outbreaks accounts for approximately $8.6 billion per year.

In order to stay safe and protected, it is of significant importance for you to have the knowledge of some primary characteristics of fire. These include;

- Since it may spread quickly, you may not get enough time to collect your valuables or make phone calls to your friends or family members. In a matter of minutes it can become life threatening and engulf your entire residence.

- The smoke and heat that are produced as a result of fire can prove to be more dangerous than the raging flames. Inhalation of smoke can cause severe damage to your lungs and the poisonous gases that are produced as a result can make you drowsy and disoriented.
- Research suggests that in comparison to deaths caused by burn injuries, more people die due to oxygen deficiency.

Prepping for a Fire Outbreak (Precautionary Measures)

- It is important to install smoke alarms as they can decrease your chances of dying due to fire by warning you in the event of a fire outbreak.
- It is essential that these alarms are installed at different levels of your residence.
- Additionally, you need to clean and test these alarms at least once a month. To keep them in a working condition, it is important that the batteries are replaced at least once a year.
- Review the escape route (that you may have to use in case of a fire outbreak). Make sure that the security railings on the windows can be opened easily from the inside. In case your residence is equipped with strong security mechanisms from the outside, you can consider using security ladders for your escape.

- Keep your storage area clean. Do not let trash such as magazines and newspapers accumulate in the storage area.
- It is important that you do not use flammable liquids such as naphtha, benzene and gasoline indoors. In case you need to store these liquids indoors, take proper precautionary measures to ensure your safety and security.
- Smoking in the area where these liquids are stored is strongly prohibited.
- When using alternative heating sources, be very careful.
- Heaters should be placed at least three to four feet away from materials that can catch fire. Properly insulate the walls and floors nearby.
- It is important to shield the fireplace using a screen.
- It is important to keep lighters and matches away from the reach of children in a secure place.
- It is important to get your heating units inspected and cleaned annually by a certified technician/specialist.
- Additionally, it is important that you do not smoke in your bed, or when you are feeling drowsy or sleepy. Always use sturdy ashtrays. It is also important to dispose-off cigarette butts properly to avoid any incident.
- It is also important to get the electrical wiring of your residence checked by a professional electrician. Make sure that the loose plugs or exposed wires are covered properly with cover plates. It is also important to ensure that the wiring does not run under the rugs or other high traffic areas of your residence.

- It is also important that you do not overload extension cords or outlets. In case you need to plug in more than one applications in an electrical outlet, you need to get a UL- approved unit installed that has built in circuit breakers for the purpose of preventing short circuits and sparks.
- It is important to get fire extinguishers installed in your residence. Additionally, it is important for you to teach your family members about using these in the event of a fire outbreak.
- To enhance your safety and security, you can consider installing automatic fire sprinkling system in your home/apartment.

During a Fire (Precautionary Measures)

- If the event your clothes catch fire, do not panic. Drop and roll until the fire is extinguished. Remember running will not do any good. It only makes the fire burn faster.
- To escape a fire, you need to check closed doors (to make sure they are not overheated) before you open them. If you need to escape through a closed door, you can use the back of your hands to feel the top of the door, the door knob, and the crack between the door and also the door frame before you try to open it.
- Make sure that you do not use the palm of your hands to check these. In case you burn your palms, your

ability to escape a fire may be impaired (you may find it difficult to climb ladders or crawl).

- In order to delay the spread of fire, it is important that you close the doors behind you when escaping.
- Once you have escaped successfully and are successfully out, do not run. Call 9-1-1 and wait for the help to arrive.

After a Fire

In the period following a fire, it is important that you follow the guidelines mentioned below;

- If any of your family members have received burn injuries, or you are a burn victim yourself, call 9-1-1. Cool your burns and cover the burns to reduce the chances of catching an infection or further injuries.
- If you detect smoke and heat, when you enter a building, it is important to evacuate immediately.
- If you have a safe or some strong box made of metal do not try to open it for several hours, as it may still be holding extreme heat.

Earthquake

An earthquake is one of the most destructive and frightening phenomena of nature that can cause severe damage and destruction. It is caused by the sudden release of strain that has accumulated over a long period of time which causes the earth to shake.

The plate tectonics of the Earth have kept it in shape for millions of years since the plates forming the surface of the earth move slowly under, over and past each other. This movement is very slow and gradual. But when the plates become locked together, they are unable to release the accumulating energy, and when this accumulating energy grows strong enough, these plates break free causing the earth to shake with immense force.

Prepping for an Earthquake

- Get the defensive electrical wiring, leaky gas lines and inflexible utility connections repaired to minimize damage (you need to take professional help to get the job done).

- It is important that you place heavy or large objects on lower shelves. Fasten shelves, large picture frames and mirrors to the walls and keep the top heavy
- objects supported.
- Additionally, keep bottled foods, glassware and other breakables in lower cabinets or shelves. Keep them fastened securely.
- It is also of significant importance to keep the overhead lighting fixtures anchored.
- It is also important for you to make sure that you install flexible pipe fittings in your residence in order to avoid water leaks and gas leaks. In addition to offering greater security, these fittings are more resistant to breakage.
- As a precautionary measure, locate safe spots in your residence such as a sturdy table under which you can take refuge in the event of an earthquake.
- It is also important to hold regular drills with your family members to make sure that each of them is well informed to combat a crisis situation.

During an Earthquake

- During an earthquake, it is important that you limit your movements to a few steps to a nearby safe place. It is important to stay indoors until the shaking has stopped and you are sure that the exit is safe.
- If you are indoors when an earthquake strikes,
  1. Take shelter under a heavy and sturdy piece of furniture. However, if there is no piece of furniture

near you, under which you can hide, cover your head and face with your arms and crouch in an inside corner of the building.

2. It is also important to stay away from outside doors, walls and windows or anything that could fall, break and cause damage.

3. Stay in bed if you are there when an earthquake strikes-hold and protect your head using a pillow (make sure you are not under a heavy light fixture that could fall upon you and cause damage.

4. In case you choose to use a doorway for shelter, it is important to make sure that it is in close proximity to you and if you think it is strongly supported doorway.

5. You need to stay inside your residence until the shaking has stopped. And it is safe to go outside. Most injuries during an earthquake occur when people are hit by falling objects when entering or exiting from buildings.

6. It is also important to be aware that there may be a power outage (be prepared for that).

7. It is also important that you do not use the elevators to escape.

8. If you are standing under a building, utility wires or street lights, step away.

9. If you are in a moving vehicle, stop as quickly as possible. Do not step out of your car. Avoid stopping near trees, buildings and overpasses.

10. Proceed cautiously once the earthquake has stopped. Watch out for bridge or road damage.

11. If you are trapped under debris, do not make a mistake of lighting a match.
12. It is also important that you do not panic or try to kick up dust.
13. Cover your mouth using a clothing or handkerchief to avoid dust getting into your lungs.
14. In case you are trapped inside your house or building, tap on a wall so that rescue teams can locate you. Shout only as your last resort as it can cause you to inhale dangerous amounts of dust.
15. If your area is struck by an earthquake, be prepared for the after-shocks.

After an Earthquake

1. Stay away from the affected area unless your assistance has been specifically requested by fire, police or relief organizations.
2. It is important that you open the cabinets safely as some objects may fall off from shelves and cause damage.
3. If your local authority issues a tsunami warning, know that a series of dangerous waves is on its way that can cause serious damage. If you live near a coastal area, stay away from beach.

Tornados

Tornadoes are nature's most violent storms. Spawned from powerful thunderstorms, tornadoes can cause fatalities and devastate a neighborhood in seconds. A tornado appears as a rotating, funnel-shaped cloud that extends from a thunderstorm to the ground with whirling winds that can reach 300 miles per hour. Damage paths can be in excess of one mile wide and 50 miles long. Every state is at some risk from this hazard. Some tornadoes are clearly visible, while rain or nearby low-hanging clouds obscure others. Occasionally, tornadoes develop so rapidly that little, if any, advance warning is possible.

Before a tornado hits, the wind may die down and the air may become very still. A cloud of debris can mark the location of a tornado even if a funnel is not visible. Tornadoes generally occur near the trailing edge of a thunderstorm. It is not uncommon to see clear, sunlit skies behind a tornado.

In order to stay protected, you need to understand the following basic facts about tornadoes.

- They may strike quickly, with little or no warning.
- They may appear nearly transparent until dust and debris are picked up or a cloud forms in the funnel.
- The average tornado moves Southwest to Northeast, but some tornadoes have been known to move in any direction.
- The average forward speed of a tornado is 30 MPH, but may vary from stationary to 70 MPH.
- Tornadoes can accompany tropical storms and hurricanes as they move onto land.
- Waterspouts are tornadoes that form over water.
- Tornadoes are most frequently reported east of the Rocky Mountains during spring and summer months.
- Peak tornado season in the southern states is March through May; in the northern states, it is late spring through early summer.
- Tornadoes are most likely to occur between 3 p.m. and 9 p.m., but can occur at any time.

Prepping for a Tornado

- Listen to Nationwide Network of radio stations or to commercial television or radio newscasts for the latest information.
- You need to stay informed for approaching storms.
- Keep a check on dangerous signs like a large hail, dark, often greenish sky or a large, dark, low lying cloud.
- If you see any of these signs and approaching storms or any of the danger signs, be prepared to take shelter immediately.

During a Tornado

If you are under a Tornado Warning, take into consideration the following safety measures,

- A structure (e.g. residence, small building, school, nursing home, hospital, factory, shopping center, high-rise building), go to a pre-designated shelter area such a safe room, basement, storm cellar, or the lowest building level. If there is no basement, go to the center of an interior room on the lowest level.
- If you are in a vehicle, truck, trailer or mobile home get out immediately and go to the lowest floor of a sturdy, nearby building or a storm shelter.
- If you are outdoors with no shelter, lie flat in a nearby ditch or depression and cover your head with your hands.
- Be aware of the potential for flooding.
- Do not get under an overpass or bridge. You are safer in a low, flat location.
- Never try to outrun a tornado in congested areas in a car or truck. Instead, leave the vehicle immediately for safe shelter.
- Watch out for flying debris. Flying debris from tornadoes causes more fatalities and injuries.

Floods

Floods are one of the most common hazards in the United States.

Prepping for a Flood

To prepare for a flood, you should:

- Avoid building in a floodplain unless you elevate and reinforce your home.
- Elevate the furnace, water heater, and electric panel if susceptible to flooding.
- Install "check valves" in sewer traps to prevent flood water from backing up into the drains of your home.
- Construct barriers (levees, beams, floodwalls) to stop floodwater from entering the building.
- Seal walls in basements with waterproofing compounds to avoid seepage. During a Flood If a flood is likely in your area, you should:

27

- Listen to the radio or television for information.
- Be aware that flash flooding can occur. If there is any possibility of a flashflood, move immediately to higher ground. Do not wait for instructions to move.
- Be aware of streams, drainage channels, canyons, and other areas known to flood suddenly. Flash floods can occur in these areas with or without such typical warnings as rain clouds or heavy rain.
- If you must prepare to evacuate, you should do the following:
  - Secure your home. If you have time, bring in outdoor furniture. Move essential items to an upper floor.
  - Turn off utilities at the main switches or valves if instructed to do so. Disconnect electrical appliances. Do not touch electrical equipment if you are wet or standing in water.

If you have to leave your home, remember these evacuation tips:

• **Do not walk through moving water.** Six inches of moving water can make you fall. If you have to walk in water, walk where the water is not moving. Use a stick to check the firmness of the ground in front of you.
• **Do not drive into flooded areas.** If floodwaters rise around your car, abandon the car and move to higher ground if you can do so safely. You and the vehicle can be quickly swept away.

After a Flood

- Listen for news reports to learn whether the community's water supply is safe to drink.
- Avoid floodwaters; water may be contaminated by oil, gasoline, or raw sewage.
- Water may also be electrically charged from underground or downed power lines.
- Avoid moving water.
- Be aware of areas where floodwaters have receded. Roads may have weakened and could collapse under the weight of a car.
- Stay away from downed power lines, and report them to the power company.
- Return home only when authorities indicate it is safe.
- Stay out of any building if it is surrounded by floodwaters.
- Use extreme caution when entering buildings; there may be hidden damage, particularly in foundations.
- Service damaged septic tanks, cesspools, pits, and leaching systems as soon as possible. Damaged sewage systems are serious health hazards.
- Clean and disinfect everything that got wet. Mud left from floodwater can contain sewage and chemicals.

Hurricanes

A hurricane is a type of tropical cyclone, the generic term for a low pressure system that generally forms in the tropics. A typical cyclone is accompanied by thunderstorms, and in the Northern Hemisphere, a counterclockwise circulation of winds near the earth's surface.

All Atlantic and Gulf of Mexico coastal areas are subject to hurricanes or tropical storms. Parts of the Southwest United States and the Pacific Coast experience heavy rains and floods each year from hurricanes spawned off Mexico. The Atlantic hurricane season lasts from June to November, with the peak season from mid-August to late October.

Hurricanes can cause catastrophic damage to coastlines and several hundred miles inland. Winds can exceed 155 miles per hour. Hurricanes and tropical storms can also spawn tornadoes and microbursts, create storm surges along the coast, and cause extensive damage from heavy rainfall.

Hurricanes are classified into five categories based on their wind speed, central pressure, and damage potential (see chart). Category Three and higher hurricanes are considered major hurricanes, though Categories One and Two are still extremely dangerous and warrant your full attention.

Hurricanes can produce widespread torrential rains. Floods are the deadly and destructive result. Slow moving storms and tropical storms moving into mountainous regions tend to produce especially heavy rain. Excessive rain can trigger landslides or mud slides, especially in mountainous regions. Flash flooding can occur due to intense rainfall. Flooding on rivers and streams may persist for several days or more after the storm.

Prepping for a Hurricane

To prepare for a hurricane, you should take the following measures:

- Make plans to secure your property. Permanent storm shutters offer the best protection for windows. A second option is to board up windows with 5/8" marine plywood, cut to fit and ready to install. Tape does not prevent windows from breaking.
- Install straps or additional clips to securely fasten your roof to the frame structure. This will reduce roof damage.
- Be sure trees and shrubs around your home are well trimmed.
- Clear loose and clogged rain gutters and downspouts.
- Determine how and where to secure your boat.
- Consider building a safe room.

During a Hurricane

- Listen to the radio or TV for information.
- Secure your home, close storm shutters, and secure outdoor objects or bring them indoors.
- Turn off utilities if instructed to do so. Otherwise, turn the refrigerator thermostat to its coldest setting and keep its doors closed.
- Turn off propane tanks.

- Avoid using the phone, except for serious emergencies.
- Moor your boat if time permits.
- Ensure a supply of water for sanitary purposes such as cleaning and flushing toilets. Fill the bathtub and other large containers with water.

You should evacuate under the following conditions:

- If you are directed by local authorities to do so. Be sure to follow their instructions.
- If you live in a mobile home or temporary structure—such shelters are particularly hazardous during hurricanes no matter how well fastened to the ground.
- If you live in a high-rise building—hurricane winds are stronger at higher elevations.
- If you are unable to evacuate, go to your wind-safe room. If you do not have one,
- follow these guidelines:
  - Stay indoors during the hurricane and away from windows and glass doors.
  - Close all interior doors—secure and brace external doors.
  - Keep curtains and blinds closed. Do not be fooled if there is a lull; it could be the eye of the storm—winds will pick up again.
  - Take refuge in a small interior room, closet, or hallway on the lowest level.
  - Lie on the floor under a table or another sturdy object.

Thunderstorms and Lightning

Despite their small size, thunderstorms can be dangerous. Irrespective of their size, every thunderstorm produces lighting. According to an estimate, lightning injures more than 300 people each year and kills more than 80 people in the Unites States. Even though most of these survive, people that are struck by lightning commonly report a wide range of long-term, debilitating symptoms.

Other dangers that are associated with thunderstorms include; strong winds, flash flooding, hail and tornadoes. Among these flash flooding is responsible for more deaths compared to other hazards associated with thunderstorms. In the Western United States, dry thunderstorms that do not produce rain are more common or prevalent. Whilst these thunderstorms do not produce rains as the falling drops of rain evaporate before reaching the ground, they are still dangerous because lightning produced by dry thunderstorms can still reach the ground and start wildfires.

In order to stay protected, you need to understand the following basic facts about thunderstorms and lightning.

- Thunderstorms may occur either singly, in lines or in clusters.
- Typically thunderstorms produce heavy rains for brief periods that may last from 30 minutes to about an hour.
- For the development of thunderstorms warm, humid conditions are highly favorable.
- Approximately ten percent of thunderstorms are classified as severe. Typically severe thunderstorms are the ones that produce hail (about 3 quarters of an inch in diameter) produce winds of 58 miles per hour and produce a tornado.
- The unpredictability of lightning increases the risk to property and individuals.
- It often strikes outside of heavy rain and may occur as far as ten miles away from any rainfall.
- Most injuries and fatalities occur when people are caught outdoors in the summer months during the evening and the afternoon.
- Though your chances of being struck by lightning are estimated to be 1 in 600,000, it can be further reduced by following some safety precautions that are described below.
- It is also important for you to understand that lightning victims carry no electrical charge and should be attended to immediately.

Prepping for Lightning and Thunderstorms

In order to prepare for a thunderstorm, following measures need to be taken. These include;

- Remove the branches and leaves of dead or rotting trees as they could fall during a severe thunderstorm and cause severe damage or injury.
- You need to remember the 30/30 lightning safety rule. If one cannot count to 30 after seeing lightning and after hearing thunder, it is safe to stay indoors. In order to ensure safety, it is essential to stay indoors for 30 minutes after hearing thunder.

During Lightning and Thunderstorms

Following is a list of guidelines you need to follow when your area is likely to be affected by lightning and thunderstorm.

- Cancel or postpone all your outdoor activities.
- It is safe to stay indoors. Take refuge in a building, home, or your vehicle. Even though, you may be injured when your vehicle is struck by lightning, you are much safer in a vehicle than outside.
- It is important for you to remember that rubber soled shoes or rubber tires provide no protection from lightning. Nevertheless, if your vehicle is hard toped, its steel body offers increased protection provided you are not touching any metal.
- Additionally, it is important that you secure all outdoor objects that may cause damage or could blow away.
- To ensure safety, it is important to keep your windows and outside doors shut. If your windows are not secured by shutters, close all the blinds, shades and curtains.
- It is important to avoid bathing or showering as bathroom fixtures and plumbing are good conductors of electricity.

- Remember use a corded phone only for emergencies. Cellular phones and cordless phones are safe to be used.
- Unplug all electrical appliances such as air conditioners, computers and other items as power surges from lightning can cause serious damage.
- Keep yourself updated using a battery operated NOAA Weather Radio.

If your area is likely to be affected by lightning, avoid the following;

- Natural rods of lightning like isolated trees in an open area.
- Open fields such as hilltops, beaches etc.
- Small structures or isolated sheds in open areas.
- All metals such as tractors, motorcycles, bicycles etc.

Additionally, if someone is struck by lightning, it is important to call 9-1-1 as soon as possible for medical assistance. In case you attempt to give first aid to a victim of lightning (while you wait for the help to arrive), carefully follow the following guidelines.

- **Mouth to Mouth Resuscitation:** If the victim has stopped breathing, begin mouth to mouth resuscitation.
- **CPR:** If the victim's heart has stopped beating, administer CPR.
- **Check for Pulse:** If you can still feel the pulse of a lightning victim, and he is still breathing, look for

other injuries. Check for burns, broken bones, loss of hearing and eyesight. Be prepared for the nervous system damage.

Volcanic Eruptions

A volcano is an opening in the surface of the earth through which lava or molten rocks escape to the surface of the earth. When the pressure of gases within these rocks becomes great, it causes the volcanic lava ashes and gases to escape with immense pressure. This eruption can be explosive or quiet. During a volcanic eruption, poisonous gases may leak, there may also be flying rocks and ash. Because of intense heat, lava flows are great fire hazards. Whilst they destroy everything in their path, lava flows very slowly giving people adequate time to move out of the way.

Additionally, fresh volcanic ash that is made of pulverized rock can be acidic, abrasive gassy, gritty and odorous. Whilst it does not pose serious threats to adults, the ash and acidic gases can cause serious lung damage to small infants to elderly and to individuals with respiratory problems/illnesses.

Additionally, volcanic ash can also cause damage to machinery including electrical equipment and engines. When these ash accumulations mix with water they become heavy-heavy enough to collapse roofs. Volcanic eruptions can be accompanied by other natural hazards such as flash floods, earthquakes, acid rain and landslides. Under special conditions it can also cause tsunamis.

In the United States, active volcanoes can be found in Alaska, the Northwest, the Pacific Northwest and Hawaii.

Prepping for a Volcanic Eruption

- Before a volcanic eruption, it is essential that you add a pair of goggles and breathing mask to your supplies disaster kit, for each member of your family.
- To stay safe, it is important to stay away from active volcano sites.

During a Volcanic Eruption:

In case a volcano erupts in your area, remember the following guidelines,

- In order to avoid hot gases, lava flow, flying debris and lateral blast, it is important to evacuate the danger zone immediately.
- It is important for you to be aware of mudflows. The danger from these flows increase with heavy rains especially near stream channels. It is also important for you to remember that a mudflow moves very fast-faster than you can walk. So, if you have to cross a bridge during evacuation and the mud flow is approaching, do not cross the bridge.

- It is important for you to wear long pants and long sleeved shirts that cover your body completely.
- To protect your eyes, wear goggles. Additionally, if you are suffering from weak eyesight, wearing eye glasses is a safer option than wearing contacts.
- In order to stay protected from the volcanic ash, it is essential to stay away from areas that are at a lower level from the volcano.
- Until the ash has settled, it is safe to stay indoors. Nevertheless, if there is a danger of roof collapse, evacuate your residence immediately and move to a safer location.
- Close all the windows, doors and other ventilations such as chimneys, air conditioners, vents, and furnaces).
- To ensure safety, it is important to clear heavy ash from low pitched or flat roofs and rain gutters.
- It is also important for you to avoid driving in heavy ash fall unless it is inevitable. If you cannot avoid driving, drive very slowly and carefully.

Landslides and Debris Flow

All territories and States in the United States are vulnerable to landslides. In a landslide, heavy masses of earth, rock or debris can slide down a slope. Landslides can be triggered by volcanic eruptions, earthquakes, fires and storms.

Mudflows and debris are rivers of earth, rock and other debris that gets saturated with water. These develop when water rapidly accumulates in the ground during heavy rainfall or snowmelt which converts the earth into a flowing river of slurry or mud.

Landslides can flow rapidly and strike with no warning at the speed of an avalanche. These can travel several miles from their source and grow in size as they pick up cars, boulders and other materials.

The problems due to landslide can be caused due to mismanagement of land, particularly in coastal and rocky areas. Professional inspections, proper design and zoning can minimize the incidents of landslide, debris and mudflow.

Prepping for a Landslide

In order to stay protected from landslides, debris flow or mudflow, it is important for you to remember the following guidelines;

- Avoid building your residence close to mountain edges, near steep slopes or natural drainage ways.
- In order to get expert advice on corrective measures, it is of paramount importance to consult a professional.
- To reduce the risk of hazards, it is important to have sturdy pipe fittings installed to avoid water or gas leaks.

Understanding the Warning Signs of Landslide

- Before landslide, you may notice some changes in your landscape such as land movement, leaning trees, small slides, and storm water drainage on slopes.
- Your windows or doors may become stuck.
- You may notice the appearance of new cracks in bricks, plaster or tiles.
- You may also begin to notice cracks appearing on the ground, on paved areas such as driveways or streets.
- If the underground utility lines break without any reason, it might be a warning sign of a landslide.
- Most commonly a faint reverberating sound is noticeable before a landslide occurs. (The sound gradually increases in volume).
- In addition, a bulging ground appears at the base of a slope as the landslide nears.
- Another common warning sign is the breakage of ground water to the surface.

- The ground slopes downward in one direction and may begin shifting in the same direction as your feet.
- You may also hear some unusual sounds such as the cracking of trees which might indicate the movement of debris.

During a Debris Flow/Landslide:

Additionally, it is essential for you to follow the guidelines mentioned below If a debris flow or landslide occurs,

- To stay safe, it is important that you step away from the path of a debris flow or landslide as quickly as possible.
- In case you are unable to escape, curl yourself into a tight ball and protect your head.

After a Debris Flow/Landslide:

Additionally, after a debris flow or landslide occurs, it is important to take into consideration following guidelines;

- Step away from the affected area as there may be an increased danger of additional slides.
- Check for injured or trapped people near the affected area and guide the members of the rescue team in their rescue operation. Avoid entering into the affected area directly.
- It is important to look out for associated dangers of landslide such as broken utility (electricity, water and sewage) lines and damaged railways and roadways.

- Additionally, it is of significant importance to reconstruct the damaged ground as soon as possible since erosion caused by the loss of ground can trigger flash flooding and additional landslides in the near future.
- In order to reduce the risk of a landslide, it is important to seek the advice of an expert or a geo technical expert who can evaluate landslide hazards and design corrective techniques to minimize potential risk.

Tsunamis

Also known as seismic sea waves, Tsunamis are a series of gigantic waves that are created by an underwater disturbance such as volcanic eruption, landslide or an earthquake. The enormous Tsunami waves can move hundreds of miles per hour in the open ocean and smash into land with enormous strength. The Tsunami waves can be as high as 100 feet.

From the point where the Tsunami originates, gigantic waves travel outward in all directions. As the wave approaches the coastline, it increases in height. The size of the wave is influenced greatly by the topography of the ocean floor or the coastline. It is also important to remember that multiple waves may be produced as a result of Tsunami and succeeding waves may be larger than the first wave hitting the shore.

This is the reason why a small tsunami wave that hits the shore at one point can be a giant wave a few miles away. All tsunamis are potentially dangerous even though they do not cause same amount of damage on very coastline they strike.

A tsunami is most commonly generated by the earthquake induced movement of the ocean. If a major landslide or earthquake occurs close to the shore, the first wave in a series could reach the beach in a few minutes even before a warning can be issued.

Areas that are at a greater risk of getting affected by Tsunamis are the ones that are less than 25 feet above sea level and fall within a mile of the coastline. Deaths in a Tsunami mostly occur due to drowning. Other hazards due to Tsunami include fire outbreak from broken utility lines, flooding and contamination of drinking water.

Prepping for a Tsunami:

- Especially if you are in a coastal area, turn on your radio to stay informed about a Tsunami warning or an earthquake warning.
- It is also important to move to a higher ground and remain there until it is safe.

Tsunami-Nature's Warning

If you notice a clear recession in water, it is best to stay away from the coastline. This is nature's indication of Tsunami and it should be paid attention to. You need to move away immediately.

During a Tsunami:

Evan after a Tsunami, you need to follow certain guidelines to stay protected. These include;

- Stay away from the damaged or flooded area until the area is declared as safe by official authorities.
- It is of paramount importance to stay away from debris in the water due to safety reasons.

Prepping for Technological Hazards

Hazardous Material Incidents

A number of communities have Local Emergency Planning Committees (LEPC). The responsibilities of these communities include collection of information about hazardous materials in the community and making sure that this information is available to general public upon request.

These Local Emergency Planning Committees also have this additional responsibility of developing and designing emergency plans for chemical emergencies that may take place in a community. Communicating the risks of chemical emergencies are an important part of the plan.

In order to find out more about chemical hazards and the measures that can be taken to minimize the risk to individuals and community from these materials, you can contact your local emergency management office in order to obtain contact information on your local emergency planning committee. It is also essential to add the following supplies to your disaster supplies kit including;

- A duct tape
- A pair of scissors, and
- Plastic sheeting

During a Hazardous Material Incident:

During a hazardous material incident, it is essential to follow the guideline mentioned below;

- For detailed information and instructions, listen to your local radio or television stations.
- In order to minimize the risk of contamination stay away from the area. You need to remember that some toxic chemicals are odorless so it is safe to stay away from the affected area.
- Additionally, if your local emergency planning committee asks you
  1. To evacuate, you need to do so immediately.
  2. If you are requested to stay indoors, keep the doors and windows locked. Keep all the fireplace dampers, doors and vents closed.
  3. Additionally, it is important to turn off the ventilation systems and air conditioners. In large buildings, it is important to set ventilation systems on a recirculation so that no outside air is drawn into the building. If this is not possible, it is essential to turn off the ventilation systems.

4. It is important for you to have a shelter room. This should be above the ground and have very few openings to the outside.
5. To stay safe, it is important to seal all the doors, windows and vents using plastic sheeting and duct tape.

After a Hazardous Material Incident:

Additionally, after a hazardous material incident, it is important for you to remember the following guidelines;

- Return home only when authorities declare it is safe to do so. Open all the doors, windows and vents to provide ventilation.
- If you have accidently come in contact with or exposed to hazardous chemicals, it is important to act quickly.

1. Follow decontamination instructions from local authorities. You might be asked by the authorities to take a thorough shower or to follow certain procedures or protocols such as staying away from water etc.
2. In case you notice unusual symptoms, seek medical treatment as soon as possible.
3. It is of paramount importance to put the shoes/clothing etc that have been exposed to chemicals in a tightly sealed container. It is essential that you do not let these materials come in contact with other materials. To properly

dispose-off these materials, it is important to contact your local authorities.

4. It is important to inform everyone who comes in contact with you that you have been exposed to a toxic substance.

5. To obtain expert advice on how to clean up your land and property, it is important to contact your local authority.

6. If you notice any unusual change in the environment, inform your local authorities.

Household Chemical Incidents/Emergencies:

Before a Household Chemical Incident:

The following are guidelines need to be followed for buying and storing hazardous household chemicals safely:

- Buy only as much of a chemical as you think you will use. Leftover material can be shared with neighbors or donated to a business, charity, or government agency.
- Keep products containing hazardous materials in their original containers and never remove the labels unless the container is corroding. Corroding containers should be repackaged and clearly labeled.
- Never store hazardous products in food containers.
- Never mix household hazardous chemicals or waste with other products.
- Incompatibles, such as chlorine bleach and ammonia, may react, ignite, or explode.

Take the following precautions to prevent and respond to accidents:

- Follow the manufacturer's instructors for the proper use of the household chemical.
- Never smoke while using household chemicals.
- Never use hair spray, cleaning solutions, paint products, or pesticides near an open flame. Although you may not be able to see or smell them, vapor particles in the air could catch fire or explode.
- Clean up any chemical spill immediately. Use rags to clean up the spill. Wear gloves and eye protection. Allow the fumes in the rags to evaporate outdoors, then dispose of the rags by wrapping them in a newspaper and placing them in a sealed plastic bag in your trash can.
- Dispose of hazardous materials correctly. Take household hazardous waste to a local collection program. Check with your county or state environmental or solid waste agency to learn if there is a household hazardous waste collection program in your area.

During a Household Chemical Incident/Emergency:

If there is a danger of fire or explosion:

- Get out of the residence immediately. Do not waste time collecting items or calling the fire department when you are in danger. Call the fire department from outside (a cellular phone or a neighbor's phone) once you are safely away from danger.

- Stay upwind and away from the residence to avoid breathing toxic fumes.
- If someone has been exposed to a household chemical:
    1. Find any containers of the substance that are readily available in order to provide requested information. Call emergency medical services.
    2. Follow the emergency operator or dispatcher's first aid instructions carefully. The first aid advice found on containers may be out of date or inappropriate.
    3. Do not give anything by mouth unless advised to do so by a medical professional.
    4. Discard clothing that may have been contaminated. Some chemicals may not wash out completely.

Preparing for the Unthinkable

Nuclear Power Plant Threats/Incidents

Prepping for a Nuclear Power Plant Incident:

Before a nuclear power plant emergency/incident, it is essential to obtain public emergency information materials from the power company that Emergency operates your local nuclear power plant or your local emergency services office.

In case you live within 10 miles of the power plant, you should receive these materials yearly from the power company or your state or local government.

During a Nuclear Power Plant Incident:

The following are guidelines for what you should do if a nuclear power plant emergency occurs.

- If you are asked to evacuate, Keep car windows and vents closed; use re-circulating air.
- On the other hand, if you are advised to stay indoors, it is important to,
  1. Turn off all the fans, vents, furnaces or other sources through which air can get in.
  2. It is important not to use phone unless it is absolutely necessary to use a phone.
- If you suspect that you have been exposed to nuclear radiation,

  1. Change your clothes immediately and remove your shoes.
  2. Put exposed clothing in a plastic bag.
  3. Seal the bag and place it out of the way.
  4. Take a thorough shower.

After a Nuclear Power Plant Incident:

Moreover, after a nuclear power plant incident, it is important to seek medical treatment for any unusual symptoms that you suspect may be related to radiation exposure.

Medicine, Emergency, Survival Kits and Tools

Assemble a Disaster Supplies Kit

Having a disaster supply kit ready to take with you at a moment's notice ensures that you will have necessary supplies no matter how fast you may need to evacuate. Pack supplies in duffel bags or backpacks and keep them in a designated place. Your kit will also come in handy if you must take shelter in your home. This list will help ensure that your disaster supply kit includes all the essentials.

1. **Water:**

- Pack at least one gallon per person per day for at least three days.
- Store water in tightly sealed, non-breakable plastic, fiberglass or enamel-lined metal containers.
- Change your water every six months.

2. **Food:**

- Pack enough food to last each family member at least three days.
- Include canned and boxed foods because they require little preparation and stay good for long periods of time. Remember to bring a manual can opener or to buy food in self-opening cans.
- Pack foods in sealed metal or plastic containers.
- Replace food every six months.
- Include foods for infants and family members with special diets.

3. Equipment and Supplies:

When assembling your disaster supplies kit, you need to ensure that it contains the following equipment and supplies. These include (but not limited to);

- Battery Powered Radio
- Flashlights
- Spare batteries
- Plastic bags (re-sealable)
- Towels and washcloths
- Garbage bags
- Sleeping bags and blankets
- Paper plates, cups and plastic utensils
- Toothpaste, shampoo, important toiletries and toothbrushes
- Extra clothing and shoes

4. Personal Items:
- Copies of birth and marriage certificates, inventory of household goods, bank account numbers and other important documents
- Maps
- Extra car and house keys
- Prescription medications

5. First Aid Kit Essentials
- Adhesive bandages
- Antacid
- Antibiotic ointment
- Anti-diarrhea medication

- Antiseptic
- Aspirin and non-aspirin pain reliever
- Cleansing agents (isopropyl alcohol, hydrogen peroxide, soap, germicide)
- Cotton balls
- First aid manual
- Gauze pads and roll
- Latex gloves
- Laxative
- Needle and safety pins
- Petroleum jelly
- Scissors
- Sunscreen
- Thermometer
- Tongue depressors
- Triangular bandages
- Tweezers

Emergency Planning Checklists

First Aid
Supplies

Supplies	Home (√)	Vehicle (√)	Work (√)
Adhesive bandages, various sizes			
5" x 9" sterile dressing			
Conforming roller gauze bandage			
Triangular bandages			
3" x 3" sterile gauze pads			
4" x 4" sterile gauze pads			
Roll 3" cohesive bandage			
Germicidal hand wipes or waterless, alcohol-based hand sanitizer			
Antiseptic wipes			
Pairs large, medical grade, non-latex gloves			
Tongue depressor blades			
Adhesive tape, 2" width			
Antibacterial ointment			
Cold pack			
Scissors (small, personal)			
Tweezers			
Assorted sizes of safety pins			
Cotton balls			
Thermometer			
Tube of petroleum jelly or other lubricant			
Sunscreen			
CPR breathing barrier, such as a face shield			
First aid manual			

Prescription and non-prescription drugs

Supplies	Home (√)	Vehicle (√)	Work (√)
Aspirin and non-aspirin pain reliever			
Anti-diarrhea medication			
Antacid (for stomach upset)			
Laxative			
Vitamins			
Prescriptions			
Extra eyeglasses/contact lenses			

Sanitation and Emergency Supplies

Item	(√)	Item	(√)
Washcloth and towel		Heavy-duty plastic garbage bags and ties for personal sanitation uses and toilet paper	
Towelettes, soap, hand sanitizer		Medium-sized plastic bucket with tight lid	
Tooth paste, toothbrushes		Disinfectant and household chlorine bleach	
Shampoo, comb, and brush		A small shovel for digging a latrine	
Deodorants, sunscreen		Toilet paper	
Razor, shaving cream			
Lip balm, insect repellent			
Contact lens solutions			
Mirror			
Feminine supplies			

Shelter

Taking shelter is critical in times of disaster. Sheltering is appropriate when conditions require that you seek protection in your home, place of employment, or other location where you are when disaster strikes. Sheltering outside the hazard area would include staying with friends and relatives, seeking commercial lodging, or staying in a mass care facility operated by disaster relief groups in conjunction with local authorities.

To effectively shelter, you must first consider the hazard and then choose a place in your home or other building that is safe for that hazard. For example, for a tornado, a room should be selected that is in a basement or an interior room on the lowest level away from corners, windows, doors and outside walls.

Because the safest locations to seek shelter vary by hazard, sheltering is discussed in the various hazard sections. These discussions include recommendations for sealing the shelter if the hazards warrant this type of protection.

Even though mass care shelters often provide water, food, medicine, and basic sanitary facilities, you should plan to take your disaster supplies kit with you so you will have the supplies you require. Mass care sheltering can involve living with many people in a confined space, which can be difficult and unpleasant. To avoid conflicts in this stressful situation, it is important to cooperate with shelter managers and others assisting them. Keep in mind that alcoholic beverages and weapons are forbidden in emergency shelters and smoking is restricted.

The length of time you are required to shelter may be short, such as during a tornado warning, or long, such as during a winter storm. It is important that you stay in shelter until local authorities say it is safe to leave. Additionally, you should take turns listening to radio broadcasts and maintain a 24-hour safety watch.

During extended periods of sheltering, you will need to manage water and food supplies to ensure you and your family have the required supplies and quantities.

Food Supplies

During catastrophic situations, you might have to cook using alternative cooking sources such as candle warmers, fondue pots, fireplace and chafing dishes.

- Camp stoves and charcoal grills are for outdoors use.
- In addition, commercially canned food may be eaten straight out the can without warning.
- Before heating food in a can;
  1. Remove the label,
  2. Thoroughly wash and disinfect the can.
  3. In order to disinfect the can you can use a diluted solution of one part bleach to ten parts of water.
  4. Before heating the can, make sure that it is opened.

Managing (Storing Food Supplies) Without Power

If you are compelled to manage/keep food safe without power for extended periods of time, it is important to;

- Look for alternative storage options especially for perishable items (that may deteriorate).
- You can use dry ice to keep your food safe for extended periods of time. Twenty five pounds of dry ice will keep a ten cubic foot freezer below freezing for three to four days. Nevertheless, care should be taken when handling dry ice (as it can cause severe damage). Use dry, heavy gloves when handling dry ice.

Managing Water

1. **Allow people to drink according to their needs**. Many people need even more than the average of one-half gallon, per day. The individual amount needed depends on age, physical activity, physical condition, and time of year.

2. **Never ration water unless ordered to do so by authorities**. Drink the amount you need today and try to find more for tomorrow. Under no circumstances should a person drink less than one quart (four cups) of water each day. You can minimize the amount of water your body needs by reducing activity and staying cool.

3. **Drink water that you know is not contaminated first**. If necessary, suspicious water, such as cloudy water from regular faucets or water from streams or ponds, can be used after it has been treated. If water treatment is not possible, put off

drinking suspicious water as long as possible, but do not become dehydrated.

4. **Do not drink carbonated beverages instead of drinking water.** Carbonated beverages do not meet drinking-water requirements. Caffeinated drinks and alcohol dehydrate the body, which increases the need for drinking water.

5. **Turn off the main water valves.** You will need to protect the water sources already in your home from contamination if you hear reports of broken water or sewage lines, or if local officials advise you of a problem. To close the incoming water source, locate the incoming valve and turn it to the closed position. Be sure you and other family members know how to perform this important procedure.

If you want to use the water in your pipes, allow the air to enter into plumbing by turning on the faucet in your home at the highest level. This will cause small amount of water to trickle out. After some water has trickled out, it is safe to obtain water from the lowest faucet.

Additionally, to use the water that is in your hot water tank, ensure that the gas or electricity is off. You can then open the drain at the bottom of the tank. After that turn off the water intake valve and start the water flowing. You can then turn on the hot water faucet.

It is important to refill the tank before turning the electricity or gas back on. If the gas is turned off, you might need the help of a professional to turn it back on. Treat the water quality before drinking it or using it for food washing or preparation, brushing teeth, or making ice.

In addition to having a bad taste or odor, contaminated water may contain microorganisms/germs that can cause diseases such as cholera, typhoid, hepatitis, or dysentery.

Water can be treated in many ways. Whilst none of these methods are perfect, the best solution is to use a combination of methods. Nevertheless, before using any method of treatment, allow the suspended particles to settle at the bottom. You can then strain these particles using filters or a layer of clean muslin cloth.

Make sure that you have the necessary materials in your disaster supplies kit for the chosen method of water treatment. Essentially there are three methods of water treatment. These include;

- Chlorination
- Distillation
- Boiling

These instructions are for the purpose of treating water of suspicious quality, in an emergency/catastrophic situation when you have no other reliable or clean source available or you have consumed all sources of stored water. The methods of water treatment are described below;

- **Boiling**

Boiling is perhaps the safest method for the treatment of water. To boil water, take a pot or kettle and bring it to a boil. This should be done for about a minute. Bear this in mind that some of this water will evaporate. Allow the water to cool before drinking it.

- ## Chlorination

Chlorination can be performed using household liquid bleach. This will kill all the microorganisms. When using household bleach, it is important to make sure that you use the bleach that contains 5.25 to 6.0 percent sodium hypochlorite.

It is important that you do not use scented bleaches, color safe bleaches or bleaches with added cleaners. As the potency of bleach diminishes with time, it is important that you use bleach from a freshly opened bottle.

To prepare a bleach solution, add 16 drops that is about 1/8 teaspoon of bleach per gallon of water, stir it and let it stand for about half an hour. After getting dissolved in water, you can smell a slight bleach odor. If after dissolving it, you do not feel the odor, repeat the procedure and let it stand for another fifteen minutes. If even after repeating the procedure, you cannot feel the smell of chlorine, use water from a different source.

In addition, you can use other chemicals like iodine or other water treatment products that are sold in the camping or surplus stores that do not contain 5.25 to 6.0 percent sodium hypochlorite solution as the only active ingredient. These are not recommended to be used for the purpose of water treatment.

- ## Distillation

Whilst boiling and chlorination will kill moist of the microbes in water, the process of distillation will remove the microbes that are resistant to the above mentioned methods in addition to removing heavy metals, salts and a number of other chemical impurities.

The process of distillation involves boiling of water and the collection of vapors that condense. These vapors (condensed) do not contain salt or other impurities. To begin the process of distillation, fill a pot half way with water. Tie a cup to the handle on the lid of the pot such that the cup hangs right side up when the lid is upside down. Boil the water for about twenty minutes. The water that drips from the lid into the cup is distilled water and is safe to consume or drink.

When the Electricity is Out

In Case of a Power Outage

- Practice energy conservation to help your power company avoid rolling blackouts.
- Always keep your car's fuel tank at least half full – gas stations use electricity to operate pumps.
- Know how to manually release your electric garage door.
- Protect your computer with a surge protector.
- If the power goes out, check your fuse box or circuit breaker, or contact neighbors to see if the outage is limited to your own home.
- Turn off computers, stereos, televisions and appliances you were using when the power went off. Leave one light turned on so you know when power is restored.
- Avoid opening the refrigerator and freezer doors. Food will remain fresh for up to four hours after the power goes off. If you know power outages may happen, freeze water in plastic bottles to keep food cool longer.
- If the outage is expected to last for several days or more, consider relocating to a shelter or a friend's home.

Using a Generator

- If you plan to use a generator, operate it outside only – not in the basement or garage. Do not hook it up directly to your home's wiring. Instead, connect the equipment and appliances you want to power directly to the outlets on the generator.

Planning Your Evacuation Plan

Prepare a Bug-Out-Bag

One of the best ways that you can be prepared for survival when disaster strikes, is to put together a properly developed Bug-Out-Bag. A Bug-Out-Bag is essentially a large survival kit that is packed with things that may help you survive during a disaster. Preparing a Bug-Out-Bag facilitates you to quickly grab what you need should you be forced to evacuate during a disaster.

A Perfectly prepared/packed Bug-Out Bag facilitates you to get to a safer location when disaster strikes. The survival kit includes practical ways to pack food, water, survival tools and much more. Experts suggest that your Bug-Out-Bag should contain enough supplies to last for at least three days. Since major disasters often disrupt normal life and services for more than 72 hours, it is a good idea to have a Bug-Out Bag that permits you to survive for an indefinite period of time.

When preparing a Bug-Out Bag, it is important to take into consideration any special items or needs that you might require during a catastrophic situation. Typically, the items in your Bug out Bag should include;

- Flashlights
- Shovel and Camp Axe
- A few assorted knives
- Campfire
- Assorted Knives
- Firearms and ammunition
- Multivitamins
- A first Aid kit
- Maps, Navigation compass, GPS etc
- Shelter (sleeping bags, tarp, tent etc)
- Duct Tape
- Arms and ammunition
- Water
- Cash and important documents such as ID card, SS card, Gun license, birth certificates etc).

Make an Evacuation Plan in Advance

In a disaster situation, it may be necessary to evacuate your home for several days or longer. Because disasters can strike with little or no warning, you should be prepared to leave at a moment's notice. Knowing beforehand the steps to take in case of evacuation can make a big difference.

- Contact the local emergency management office to learn evacuation routes for your area.
- Determine where you will go if your community is evacuated.

- Discuss with your family the possibility of evacuation.
- Find out your child's school evacuation policy.
- Check that your disaster supply kit is assembled and ready to go.
  - Make sure your car is filled up – fuel may be in short supply during a disaster.
- Additionally, when authorities ask you to evacuate;
  - Bring your disaster supply kit.
  - Wear sturdy shoes and clothing.
  - Unplug home electronics
  - Lock the doors and windows.
  - Turn off the main switches and valves for gas, water, electricity, if instructed.
  - Inform a friend or relative of your route.
  - Follow recommended evacuation routes. Watch for washed-out bridges, flooded areas and downed power lines.

Taking Pets with you while evacuating;

- Pets should not be left behind during a disaster, but do not risk your own safety attempting to find them if you must evacuate quickly.
- Attach ID tags to your pet with your name and address.
- Remember that most emergency shelters do not allow pets (except service animals).
- Make a list of pet shelters and of hotels that permit animals in the area you would evacuate to.
- Put together an emergency supply kit for your pet. Include things like a first aid kit, food dishes, a litter box, a leash or pet carrier, medication, food, veterinary records and water.

If You Are Going to a Public Shelter

- Be aware that alcoholic beverages, pets and weapons are not allowed in public shelters.
- Practice patience and cooperation. Sharing a space with many others can be a challenge.
- Stay in the shelter until authorities advise you it is safe to leave.

How to Manage Disaster at Home

Although you may not be asked to evacuate – and even if you are – disasters can isolate you from outside help and make it necessary for you to care for yourself for days at a time. Your disaster supply kit will contain many of the tools and supplies you need. Here are other ways to use and mage the resources you have at your home.

1. **Water**
   - Water is crucial for health and survival. If a disaster is imminent, fill pitchers, jars, buckets, water bottles and your bathtub in case your community water supply is cut off.
   - If your drinking water supply is running low, use water from ice cube trays, the water heater and toilet tanks (but not bowls). It is not safe to use the water from radiators, waterbeds or swimming pools.
   - Each person should drink at least two quarts of water each day. Drink what you need each day, and look for more water for the next day.

2. **Food**
   - Ration food supplies for everyone except children and pregnant women. Most people can survive easily on half the normal amount.
   - Avoid eating food from dented or swollen cans or food that looks or smells abnormal.
   - Use pre-prepared formula for babies.

3. **Inspecting your home for damage**

Even, if you are managing a disaster situation at home, it is important that you inspect your home for damage to ensure that you stay safe during the confinement (in case you are taking refuge in your home).

- Look for structural damage, loose or damaged electrical wires, and gas leaks before re-entering your home. If you doubt the safety of the structure, contact a professional before entering.
- Do not enter a fire-damaged house until authorities have inspected it.
- Check the refrigerator and discard spoiled food.
- To claim damages, contact your insurance agent.

Possible Emergencies and Disasters	Risk Level (None, Low, Moderate or High)	How can you reduce your risk?
NATURAL DISASTERS		
Floods		
Hurricanes		
Lightning and Thunderstorms		

Tornadoes		
Earthquakes		
Volcanic Eruptions		
Landslides		
Fire outbreaks		
Tsunamis		
TECHNOLOGICAL HAZARDS		
Hazardous Material Incidents		
Household Chemical Incidents		

THE UNTHINKABLE		
Explosions/Bomb blasts		
Chemical threats		
Biological Threats		

Conclusion

It goes without saying that disasters strike with little or no warning and can leave tremendous amount of destruction and ruin in their wake. Survivors, nevertheless; can get through even the toughest circumstances using the right information and tools. Knowing which type of disasters could affect your area will help your plan more thoroughly for the disaster.

When the earth shakes, a tornado strikes, a plane crashes or a storm hits, the survivors are viewed as the lucky ones. Had they been in the hotel across the street or in the unlucky airplane, they would have been perished. We are awestruck at the whimsy of the catastrophe. However, survival is not merely a product of fate.

Whilst the advancement in the field of science and technology may lead us to a reasonable understanding of some phenomenon, it does not unfortunately translate into an accurate prediction capability.

Knowing the steps you need to take during an emergency situation can greatly reduce the risk, danger and distress you may face in case you are confronted with such a situation. Knowing that you are prepared to face the worst will definitely help you sleep a little easier at night.

Stay Safe!

Macenzie

References

- Federal Emergency Management Agency – www.fema.gov
- U.S. Fire Administration – www.usfa.dhs.gov
- Citizen Corps – www.citizencorps.gov
- U.S. Centers for Disease Control & Prevention – www.cdc.gov
- U.S. Department of Energy – www.energy.gov
- U.S. Department of Homeland Security – www.ready.gov
- U.S. Environmental Protection Agency – www.epa.gov
- National Weather Service – www.nws.noaa.gov
- U.S. Nuclear Regulatory Commission – www.nrc.gov
- American Red Cross – www.redcross.org
- Institute for Business and Home Safety – www.disastersafety.org

www.ingramcontent.com/pod-product-compliance
Lightning Source LLC
Chambersburg PA
CBHW060204290526
45789CB00003B/1158